Songs of Crocus Hill

and Other Poems and Songs

Michael E. Murphy

Elegies   7

Eveline   8
The River   9
Memories From Mary's Purse   10
The Gemini   12
Sadie Broderick   13
Mick Aasen   14
Jack   15
His Honor   16
The Home   17
Epitaph   18

Songs of Crocus Hill   21

Communion   22
Sister Karen Wadsworth   23
Numbers and Revelations   24
Winter Dreams at the Club   25
Mr. Grindheim   26
Yo-Yo Wayne   27
Rigoletto in Ichy's Store   28
Carl Wolf   29
The Title Game   30
Peto   31
The Tutor   32
The Wake   33

Other Poems   35

Buddy   36
Polonius Takes the Putt   37
On a Rooftop in Fallujah   38
Bletchley Park   39
White Caps   40
Helen of Tuscumbia   41
Deconstruction   42
Six Seasonal Haiku   43
Thanksgiving 2008   44
The Belles of St. Bart's   45
Duvida   46
The Swan   47
Silver Lake   48
The Little Sisters of the Poor   49

and Songs   51

Acacia Memory   52
Billy's Song   53
Catherine's Song   54
The Occasional   55

Our longtime family friend, the late novelist Jon Hassler, often reminded us of the importance of writing down family stories. He said we owed it to the generations that followed us. He'd say, yes, you wouldn't think what we remember about our own pasts is all that interesting, especially to others. But do it anyway, he'd say; let others – the generations that follow us – decide how interesting our lives were. Don't we all wish, he'd ask, that our parents and grandparents had left more of themselves, and what moved them, for us to read about today?

So with Jon's admonition in mind, and having been asked over the years by family members to collect my poems for posterity, I decided that the occasion of Jane's and my 50th wedding anniversary (June 12, 2015) was the right time to get on with it. And while it's true that a collection of poems is not quite the same as a memoir in prose form, most of these poems are memoirs: The people and places they imagine are drawn from my life – family members, friends, neighbors with whom I grew up and went to school in the Crocus Hill district of St. Paul or experiences I had traveling abroad as an international lawyer.

One difference between the prose memoir and these memory poems is that there is no place in a good poem – we've been told – for direct editorial comment. As the axiom goes: the poet should simply present the scene to the reader, not tell the reader what to think about the scene. And yet there is a certain amount of editorializing in the poet's choice of subject matter and the way the subject matter is presented. (Do you think I want you to sympathize with Mr. Grindheim?)

Another difference between the prose memoir and the poem is that the author of a poem is allowed to lie; it's called poetic license. The yo-yo salesmen did perform for the neighborhood kids on the broad stoop in front of the Sweetshop at the corner of Oxford and Osceola, but "Wayne" is a made-up name to represent them all. And while Joyce was a real second-grade crush of mine, "Wayne" never tried to steal her away from me; nor could I ever have thought of Joyce as perfidious, that sweet little thing who probably didn't even know I was in love with her.

I'm not alone in believing that a poem is just another form of story – a very short, short story; and that a poem should be accessible to a public audience, not just to the poetry editors on the staff of a glossy magazine and a handful of English professors. And so these poems are mostly written in the narrative style, rather than in the abstract style that emerged during and after World Wars I and II, paralleling the development of abstract art, experimental theater and the cacophonous symphony. Thanks in significant part to the work of "accessible" poets laureate, like Ted Kooser and Billy Collins, the pendulum is swinging back toward a style of poetry that a wider public audience can again understand and enjoy.

Nor am I alone in believing that a poem needs structure. Structure imposes discipline on the poet, forces the poet to write economically, and it can give the poem a certain rhythm, a pattern for the reader to follow. So most of these poems are organized by lines that can be "scanned" either by the number of syllables per line or by the number of "feet" (stressed words or syllables) per line.   For example, "Buddy" has ten syllables per line and "Numbers and Revelations" has four feet per line.

So, too, a poem can be organized around the number of stanzas in a poem or lives per stanza. For example, "The Title Game" has seven stanzas because there are seven innings in a high school baseball game.   And "Jack" has four lines per stanza (representing the four main columns in front of The Minikahda Club in Minneapolis), except for the last stanza, which has only three lines for reasons the reader will discover.

Another word about structure: From what I've read and experienced over the years, I believe that, like any good story or play, a good poem will treat the reader to what Aristotle referred to as a "discovery" – a surprise, a revelation, an epiphany. Aristotle offers perhaps the most famous example: Oedipus' blinding discovery that, despite his best-laid plans to avoid the horror, he did after all, as the Oracle had predicted, murder his father and marry his mother. But the discovery at the end of a good story may also be a delight, as in waking from *A Midsummer Night's Dream*. Sad or glad, it's the discovery that counts. You should find both kinds of discovery in these poems.

The poems are arranged in groups: **Elegies; Songs of Crocus Hill; Other Poems; and Songs.**

Sometimes the distinction here between an Elegy and a Crocus Hill poem is blurred. For example, when I wrote "The Wake" I was imagining the send-off of a young man like my paternal great-grandfather when he emigrated from Ireland to America. He seems to be boarding a "coffin ship" in Cork, which suggests he didn't make it. But my great-grandfather did make it; and in fact his bride Mary came with him, which she doesn't do in the poem. Moreover, they weren't famine emigres; we believe they left Waterford in early 1845 (just before the famines began) for job opportunities in America. So "The Wake" is an elegy, but for a fictional Irish emigrant.

So, too, with "Peto." I imagine there a young husband's loss of his red-headed wife and mother of his children. But I wrote "Peto" long before I met my real red-headed wife, Jane, and had our four beautiful children with her. Yet "Peto" is stocked with real children and adults who were my neighbors in Crocus Hill; and the poem plays out in my back yard on Fairmount Avenue. So I grouped it with the Crocus Hill poems.

The **Other Poems** don't fall into tidy categories. A few are autobiographical: We have a cat named "Buddy;" I knew Polonius' shame on the golf course; and I had the pleasure of gazing upon "my white swan" at the Bolshoi Theater and the Slavyanskaya Hotel in Moscow.

Elegies

My mother, Catherine Eveline Broderick Murphy ("Evie"), was a career high-school English teacher. She died on April 24, 1974, after a long struggle with cancer. My father, William Patrick Murphy, resigned from the Minnesota Supreme Court a year earlier to take care of her. He died twelve years (to the day) later, on April 24, 1986. I called the elegies I wrote for "Evie and the Judge" (as they were affectionately known in our Crocus Hill neighborhood in St. Paul) "Eveline" and "The River." My parents' elegies were read at their memorial masses at St. Luke's (now St. Thomas More) Church in St. Paul.

Another person whose death deeply affected me was my mother-in-law, Mary Shaw Randolph, whom we all regarded as the Queen of Kenwood. She died on October 31, 1994. "Memories From Mary's Purse" was read at her memorial Mass at the Basilica of St. Mary in Minneapolis.

My first two grandchildren, twin boys, died at and shortly after their births in April 1998. I was asked to read "The Gemini" during a memorial service for them at Christ the King Church in Minneapolis. (The twins are also remembered in the poem on page 44.) Soon thereafter, Jane and I bought a family plot at Lakewood Cemetery in Minneapolis for this sort of eventuality. Some years later we decided to put up our own gravestone so that our "estates" wouldn't have to deal with burial questions when it came time for us to "shuffle off this mortal coil." "Epitaph" is adapted from the first verse of "Acacia Memory," the song I composed for Jane on our 35th wedding anniversary (see page 47). "Epitaph" is in the 18th century English graveyard-poetry tradition; it's an "heroic quatrain" – four basically iambic pentameter lines with an "a, b, a, b" end-rhyme scheme. (See, for example, Thomas Gray's "Elegy Written in a Country Churchyard.")

Sadie Carr Broderick was my maternal grandmother and childhood "day-care provider." She had been a school teacher in Aberdeen, South Dakota. She married Edward Broderick, who owned a saloon in Breckenridge, Minnesota, where they raised my mother and her younger brother, John Broderick. Edward died young of a stroke, so Sadie followed my mother down to the Twin Cities. Sadie is buried with Edward in St. Mary's Cemetery in Breckenridge.

In "The Home," I recall visits with my brother John, who died in 2013 after a series of strokes caused by late-onset diabetes. He's also the brother who is there with us in "His Honor."

Eveline

If April was unkind in taking gray Eveline
Before she had seen her morning glories
Breed upon the garden fence,
Before she had breathed another cup of coffee
At her kitchen table beneath the wall clock
With Bill, dressed for the office,
Reading through the morning papers, and
Little Maggi smiling through the screen
At them for company;

If April was unkind in mixing our memory and
Desire once more to see her there at morning
With such music in her cherub face
As made the spruce tree sing with cardinals
The lilacs bloom, and her children laugh
For the perfect joy of her touch;

If April stirred our roots with unkind rain,
It also left things clean and warm, a new season
She perfectly prepared for us a sunlit April morning.

The River

When the river ran high with its quick green fish,
Billy and his mates, tying flies to their lines
Leaned along its banks in the dawn and wished;
Then he'd fly to the field with his cap and glove.
He sang on the stage while his sister played,
Till Evie came to town and he settled into love.
When the river ran high with its quick green fish,
Bill and his mate made a home for our lives.

When the river grew warm in the summer sun,
We smelled cut grass and listened for the lark.
We would run so far – to the edge of day –
To watch him get off the Grand Avenue car.
His briefcase in one hand, with the other
He gathered us up to the warmth of his heart.
When the river ran warm in the evening sun,
He read us Huck Finn and smoked his cigar.

As the river collected the falling leaves,
He would read our laws and write with grace
Opinions that affected the lives we would lead.
In the fragile life of Lincoln, in the flawed
Characters of Russian novels,
He would find his points and counterpoints:
The river would collect, like falling leaves,
All unequal laws of a savage race.

When the river ran low, beneath ice and snow,
He planned their trips over drinks by the fire
Saying, Evie, your French is accented with Scotch.
After she was gone, he would lose his desire.
We followed him out to the edge of his hours,
Feeling breath, and a pulse, even after his death.
As the river ran low, we would come to know
That the life we were feeling in him was ours.

Memories From Mary's Purse

I
It was not just the grocery list
Left with her purse on their bedside table
On that late October morning – a casual
Reminder from a wife that, having
Just been bereft of half his life,
He would need, after all, to eat.

II
She may also have had in mind for us all
Another Sunday night agape:
Taking each of us in at the door
With her laugh of love, eyes bright with kindness
Moving through the glad-filled rooms
Of her home on feet so small
No prints were left in the fresh carpet.
And so we were led to her white-clothed
Silver-laden table, festooned with
Red bows and golden candelabra.
Our plates she filled with verdant greens and
Moist portions of succulent duckling
Guarded by glasses deep in Burgundy wine.

III
There were also the letters she had written,
One to a daughter after a birthday
Another to a grandchild away at school –
Letters written in the present generation
But received by them from a generation past.

IV
The girl in her past would sing and swing
To gramophone music, a dark-eyed beauty
Steering her '36 Ford through Kenwood
Streets – rumble seat filled with racquets
And friends – first to her classes at the "U"
Then off on a political campaign ride
For this candidate or that one
The luckier to have her at his side.

V

And the letters written were not all.
Orders had been placed at stores
For new samples to replace old drapes.
She had called for her daughters' help
In deciding on patterns and colors,
Not so much for the help in deciding
As for the love of more time with her daughters.

VI

And that time had begun when she and Harry –
Engineer, provider, a Randolph of Virginia –
Began growing their children, quick and
Strong, like the maples planted in their yard
That stood on that late October morning
Fixed in their own monuments of fallen leaves.
She would love and teach them all in one motion,
Saying to one considering a new job
Son, Bemis may not be your bag.

VII

And there were also the photos near her purse:
There on the Spanish Steps in Rome;
With the André Chavetons in St. Cloud, above Paris;
In Frau von Braunschweig's Frankfurt home.
Wherever she went, the Europeans invited
Her in, as though she were one of their own.

VIII

Alone now, her family gathered round
As the low October sun watched
The deciduous trees dismiss their last leaves,
As tall stars in the autumn night
Listened to the sweet keening of her children,
Keening sweetly to their mother:
May the zephyrs of dawn move softly, Mary,
Round your dreaming eyes; may you turn
Your gaze again on us and tell us
When you can, if you felt our hearts
Each leaving through that night with yours.

The Gemini

The Gemini, there in the skies that night
Disappeared at dawn
Drawn back to the light of their parents' eyes.

Sadie Broderick

Gaze upon her face
Sadie Broderick's
pale blue eyes, moist at the corners
tears of joy or grief suppressed
her lips wintered thin
considering a smile.

She poses for the camera
in her sable dress
the one she saved for special,
strands of her frayed gray hair
stray like threads on the binding
of the family bible.

Is she caught there in a
worried reverie over
their drought-browned fields
and their flood-plains home
in the Red River Valley

or is she fawning on us
in contentment with what
she and her Edward did
with the Job's hand
dealt them on the prairie?

Mick Aasen

You'd hardly ever see him up there
when you turned into the circle drive
between the sculpted hedge rows
circling the practice green.

Oh, he'd be up there all right
you could depend on it
somewhere above the green,
above the rows of red and yellow tulips.

He'd be up there standing still as an egret
in his billed cap, waiting
in a shadow, between the white columns
or sitting in his little room off the portico
waiting at the window
with the patience of a confessor.

You'd see all the others, of course
the members and their guests
in white dresses and blue blazers,
the golfers walking out to the course
(faces wistfully lifted) or walking back
(faces clouded with funereal frowns).

But you wouldn't see Mick
until you'd rolled up in front
and your door was being opened for you.
And there he'd be in his khakis and cap
stepping aside for you, giving you his
soft-spoken, 'Afternoon, Mr. Allford
or an 'Evening, Mrs. Evanson.

He'd meet you there with that deep-set
blue-eyed gaze of his, looking
straight into your very soul to see if you
too could get a kick out of sitting behind
the wheel of a red, '65 Pontiac convertible.

Yes, he'd take you in with that blue-eyed gaze
and avuncular smile that made you feel
like you'd just been welcomed
to his home for a gathering of old friends.

And after the sun had gone down
and snow had covered a darkened driveway,
you'd get a glimpse of his shadow
fleeting past the dining room windows,
then car lights circling back to the front.

Your car always seemed to roll up there
just as you'd walked out to want it,
as though he'd seen you leave your table
or knew just how long you'd be chatting
in the hallway with an old friend.
(Yes, Mick knew all about old friends.)

Again he'd hold your door for you
and send you off with his soft-spoken,
'Night Mr. Naughten, 'night Mrs. Naughten,
with that blue-eyed smile of his giving off
all the light you'd need that night.

But it was the night of July 4, 2006,
when Mick made his last run
around the circle drive. Watching the
strobing lights of the ambulance
fade away beyond the hedge rows,
one imagined Mick gazing back at us
with a shade of apology in his parting smile.

When next we gathered as old friends,
the green flag out beyond the white columns
fluttered at half-mast;
and we were holding open for one another
the doors of a church, circling Mick's family
with our arms and our helpless smiles,
whispering to ourselves and to the sunset,
Good night, Mr. Aasen.

Jack

No one, not even our khakied caddies
hiking their cleeking bags all day
along the garden green, could give you
right off the number of columns up there

posing on our lakeside acropolis
like white sentinels dressed in Doric caps;
no one, not even Jack the kitchen boy
down there on his hands and knees

eyes deep as our summer's lakes
could see what it meant to Thebes for a soldier
like him to solve the riddle of the sphinx
and flush the beast from its mountain lair.

Regard this scrapbook photo from '44
Jack, posing in Army dress
at ease – at least until his sleet-blown
flak-racked glider plowed through

the tulips in Market Garden – at least until
flushing the sulfurous beast to the Rhine
he met the medals that bore him home
here to us in Minneapolis.

And then it was Jack the Doorman
Valet for Decades, this fixture among our
columns, until the running for cars
would run down to an old soldier's job

at the Starter Desk. There, everyone
even the silvered titans, would heel to his
No sir, time's taken, sent with that brass voice
a pitch above the din of kitchen and war.

The day our age-bent Jack lay down his cane
anyone could give you the number of columns
above the garden green: one less than yesterday.

His Honor

Maybe it was the briefcase
he always carried around the corner
and down Fairmount at the end of his day
that made his thin frame lean
to that side, counterbalanced, it seemed
by the cant of his head the other way.
When he'd sing out our names and stop
to watch us, I'd start firing my hardest
fastballs ever into my brother's mitt.

On winter nights, we skated out under
the stars, flirting and chasing all over
the ice to the Chordettes and all those Fours
their voices stereoed around the snow banks,
our eyes glazed with laughter.
When I saw him up there on the wide stoop
of Radisky's store overlooking the rink,
I let Gretchen Klein catch me
and gave her back her scarf.

Age, and the incurable wounds of widowhood
rounded his shoulders, curved his spine.
My brother and I closed ranks,
lunched with him on Fridays at Kellogg Square.
He'd come through the door still leaning
to one side, head canted to the other.
When the bill came, he'd give us his old
refrain: No, boys, lunch is on me;
you can get my dinner at the Ritz.

His was a traditional funeral Mass.
There is a time for death: Ecclesiastes;
On Eagles Wings, something we all could sing;
a thoughtful eulogy from a fellow judge;
the priest's earnest reminder that Dad's
soul still lives on, a notion, I confess
I could never quite grasp, at least
until I watched my brother leaving the church,
that leaning gait, his head canted the other way.

The Home

My brother knows who I am.
He lies here in Room 310
at the rest home in Mounds Park.
His Korea and Twins caps
hang on pegs behind the door.
A white curtain separates
his side from the other guy's;
it won't contain the bad air
or the calling, all the calling.

It's Monday again and we
go over the weekend's games.
His eyes moisten and wrinkle
at the win. At the loss he
stares at me like it's my fault.

Now his stare softens to a
searching, a quizzical look
moving across my face from
place to place. I know what he's
looking for. He's looking for
his volume of Plato, back
there somewhere, buried in the
Corinthian columns of
books that frame the stone fireplace.

He's searching for it over
on the side where the family
photos and Giverny print
bridge the wall between the books
and the diamond-paned windows.

And when he finds his Plato
I know just where he means to
open it to. He means to
open it to the Phaedo,
to the last pages of the
Phaedo, to recall just how
and with what insouciance
Socrates handled that last
most mundane of all questions.

Epitaph

To the green cliffs, where the merging rivers thread
where you and I were young and lingered long
our hands joining near the gifts, you brought the bread
and your summer smile and I the wine and a song

Songs of Crocus Hill

The boundaries of St. Paul's Crocus Hill district will vary somewhat depending on who is describing it. But roughly, it spreads along Summit Avenue from about Ayd Mill Road on its western edge to Ramsey Hill on its eastern edge, and south to St. Clair. It would also include two or three streets north of Summit, again from Ayd Mill Road to about Victoria; and it would include the Ben Hill area south of St. Clair and east of Lexington. If Crocus Hill were a town, Grand Avenue between Lexington and Victoria would be its downtown. "Songs of Crocus Hill" are organized according to my age progression from pre-school through grade school and into high school.

Our neighborhood public grade school was Linwood. I attended Linwood until the third grade, when I was old enough to hike the eight blocks up to St. Luke's, our neighborhood Catholic grade school then located at Summit and Victoria (now William Mitchell College of Law). In 1951 a new St. Luke's school was built next to the church on Summit and Lexington. I graduated from that school in 1953. (In 2008, the name of St. Luke's parish – a Crocus Hill institution since 1888 – was changed to St. Thomas More, probably because so many of the mansions along Summit Avenue that used to be owned by physicians are now occupied by lawyers.) I graduated from Cretin High School in 1957. Cretin, named after St. Paul's first bishop, is at the intersection of Hamline and Randolph, well beyond Crocus Hill. But Cretin was (still is) the go-to high school for most Catholic kids in Crocus Hill. "The Title Game" plays out at Cretin (now Cretin-Derham Hall). "The Tutor" is based on my experience going back to Linwood School in retirement to help immigrant children improve their English reading and writing skills.

The first elegy I ever wrote, "Peto," was inspired not so much by a death as by anxiety over a school assignment. When I was a graduate student in the English Department at the University of Minnesota in 1963, I was lucky to get into a poetry-writing seminar taught by the great American poet and literary critic Allen Tate. Each week Mr. Tate had us write, and read to the class, a different form of poem – first a sonnet, next a villanelle, and so on until we came to the Italian sestina. Notice that the six words ending the six lines of the first stanza also end the six lines of the following five stanzas, but in alternating order. Then notice that all six of these words appear again in the final tercet. (It is almost as hard to explain the form of a sestina as it is to write one.) Mr. Tate flattered me by asking my permission to publish "Peto" in the Spring 1963 issue of *The Minnesota Review*.

Most of the children's names in Peto are borrowed from two large and lovable families who lived on either side of my parents' home on Fairmount Avenue: the Inserras and the Merrills (the name of whose baby boy, Peter, could not yet be properly pronounced by his slightly older siblings). One of the happiest memories I have from my late teens is the sound of giddy laughter echoing through our yard, as the Merrill and Inserra children chased one another across our lawns in some hide-and-seek or other game that I wished I were still young enough to play with them.

Communion

He places her in the front bedroom on Fairmount,
a choir of elms sending in pencils of sunlight.
She's in her Windsor chair, print dress of violets
on a field of gray faded and thin as her hair
the stray strands frayed like the threads on the weathered book
she reads to him. He's straddled across her wooden
footstool, now his bright motorcycle thundering
down West Seventh, the leathered girl clinging behind.

She touches her brooch; she's come to the part where the
grieving husband cradles his child on the over-
night train; or is she singing now of Lord Randal,
the brook-side rides with his perfidious lover?
Her reading, her singing, her voice seems all the same
that slight voice with its slight, revealing inflections
like the brook's, hinting at where its trout are hiding
or why the riding girl rode off with another.

Now, after their story and song, she leaves her chair
and kneels facing the vanity where he has gone
to say their Mass, placing the water glass chalice
beside the vase of flowering almond that fills
the chapel of her room with May's sweet incense.
When he turns to her for the *Ite missa est*
they hold hands, go downstairs into the kitchen and
continue their communion with cocoa and toast.

Sister Karen Wadsworth

You can laugh at this till the school bell rings
but it's true: A third-grade boy can fall in love
with the long fingers and soft, saxophone voice
of a woman in a black tunic and white wimple,
this vision of Lourdes who bathed us in her smile.

She revealed to us the mysteries of math, faith
and the whole Deuteronomic survival kit
for the children of St. Luke's parish.

And she handed us the gift of cursive writing,
her long fingers feathering the chalk in curving
clefs across the blackboard, just as
a figure skater might etch her arcs across
the ice, pirouette, like a comma, and come
to a full stop at the end of the rink: the period.

And now the arc of our lives has brought us together
again; and again I sit here before her,
this time in a room at Carondelet Village
with all its assisted living and its care for memory.
I've placed my cap, gloves and car keys
there on the lamp-table beside her.

Angled into her wheelchair, her body
forms this perfect S that balances her nodding
head with its nimbus of white hair.
She'll speak to me now in her thin voice.
I know just what she'll say:

I loved you kids; I loved the teaching,
the teaching at St. Luke's. They made me principal
at St. Matt's on the West Side and Sacred Heart
on the East Side. Then they put me in charge
of personnel. Imagine: me. But the best
was the teaching; the teaching. I loved you kids.

She repeats this sequence of office, I think,
more from her heart than from her memory.
It's time now for me to take her long fingers
between my hands. We press our cheeks together,
that last long look all across one another's face.
I take my cap and gloves and turn away.

But Michael, Michael, she calls me back, and nodding
toward the lamp-table, she says: Not even
Our Savior could start your car without those.

Numbers and Revelations

My first run-in with the mysteries of the Bible
was when I got old enough to play
touch football in the street with my brothers
and the other older kids on the block
like Sid Siegel and Mel Goldberg.
They revealed to me the rule of even
numbers on each team, unless
there were an odd number of players; then
I wouldn't count, but could play anyway
if I played on my brothers' team. The second
revelation was like and followed from the first:
On Saturdays, Sid and Mel were always
on opposite teams when a desert-yellow
bus would come and spirit them away.

Winter Dreams at the Club

Chords of *Mr. Sandman*
Lollipop, Shrimp Boats
echo over the wreaths of snow
on the houses we pass by tonight
on our way up Oxford to the Club.
An aurora borealis appears, fence-top
lights that flood the rink. We smell
the wood-burning stove, cigarette smoke
wet mittens drying on a grate.

All across the ice, a carnival of colors
screaming skaters, scarves streaming
the crack of pucks on sticks, arias
of laughter and betrayal: two boys,
neither of whom would be Henry Metzger,
brawl in the snow in front of the white
clapboard clubhouse, as Henry would say,
like ignorant armies that clash by night.

Inside, behind the wood counter
Big Ted Dwyer, bald
like a tonsured monk, takes our quarters
for the skating, our dimes for the pop
and candy, his half-smile a reminder
he'll throw us out into the black night
for fighting or cussing. Piled beneath
the benches all along the hallway walls:

the boots, skates and sticks of the families
Arth, Burke, Davis and Delaney
Eldredge, Goldberg, Haugh and Hurley
McGowan, Melady, O'Leary and Omodt
Parish, Patterson, Rogers and Rose
and Tokyo Tommy Kuhara, fastest
sprinter ever at Monroe; or as Henry
would say: Tommy could lap Achilles
in a race around the walls of Troy.

The white figure skates coming
off the ice now, chased
by a bobbing ponytail and dreaming boys,
are Judy Cormican's, the *Honeycomb*
queen of the Club. Judy sits
on a bench between her friends, Gretchen
and Molly. They laugh and share candy

and they wait for Henry, wait for him
to stride from the boys' locker room
tall on his skates and sure, hockey
on his mind, they suppose, though he may look
their way as he strides through the hall
and out to the ice, where skaters will part for him
where the lights will follow his flashing blades
where the girl he wants will find him.

For Henry too would have his dream:
to skate out under the lights,
risk a waltz jump for her,
the brown-eyed girl with the red scarf
who will glide to his side, smile, and ask him
to walk her home down Oxford
when the Club closes at ten.

Mr. Grindheim

You came from good homes around
the Club, on Osceola,
its clay courts like a beach in
summer where friends sit, gaze out;
its rink in winter all ringed
with snow, like shoulders of ice
pushed up by a North Sea storm.

I'd find some old man's chore
to take me out into my
back yard, where I'd pause to watch –
you must have thought – the tennis
or the skating, from behind
my curtain of lilac trees.

To you – new eggs, emerging
pulses of self-preservation –
I must have looked the mad ghost
whose strange language you'd hear
when I'd bark at my sullen
dog; I must have looked to you

in my baggy denim coat
catching on branches as I
moved along the fence between
my yard and the Club, a dark
specter to be by turns feared
or taunted, from a safe distance.

And, yes, I heard the taunting,
your talk of Ellis Island,
your mock Norwegian accents.
And, yet, you came from good homes;
your parents taught you to call
me – the old man who lives next
to the Club – Mr. Grindheim

as if Grindheim were a real
surname, as if Norwegian
immigrants had surnames when
we came to America,
as if Grindheim wasn't instead
a seaside town in Norway,
its name put to a new use.

I could tell you weren't bad kids;
you just hadn't lived long enough
to see the difference between
a specter haunting children
and an old man summoning
scenes from childhood: a family
skating on a pond in Grindheim.

Yo-Yo Wayne

Yo-Yo Wayne, how could I compete
with your strutting up the steps to us from your red
Plymouth convertible, your bag of Duncan yo-yos
in hand to dazzle us on the wide stoop in front of
Radisky's Linwood Sweetshop. You, in your slick
black slacks, white shirt with that yellow knit tie
your ivory smile and black, Brylcreemed hair
slicked back, eyes blue as the glass studs
on the yo-yo you played out to walk the dog
rock the cradle, loop the loop as long
as we liked, then around the world to close the sale.
The sale, at least to the older kids with paper
routes and a buck for one of your Duncan yo-yos.
I set my face to look the hard sell
but Joyce knew better. Her eyes were all over you
Wayne, and we both knew it. You knew, when you drove off
in your Plymouth convertible with your big bucks and tricks
you'd taken my Joyce from me forever; I knew it
by the way you played that guffer's knob and grinned
your ivory grin at me in your rearview mirror.

Rigoletto in Ichy's Store

The paperboy's mettle was measured by how the kid
got out there at five in the morning, kicked a fresh path
down December's snow-silenced sidewalks,
strained under the weight of the gray canvas bag
that bulged on his hip like the hump that followed Rigoletto
while he sang against the darkness of the world.

The customer's mettle was measured at dinner hour
on collection day: Would he answer the door
have the money to pay, give the kid a Christmas tip?
Ichstein was always at home on collection day.

A wizened hummel, guttural vowels in a cloud of garlic
Ichy lived behind a pair of burlap flaps at the back
of his basement store on Chatsworth. Milk right, soaps left
candy on the counter where Ichy could watch the boys
with three hands who crowded the store after school.

Don't tell me, kid, it's another month and another $3.40
you want already. You earned it. I'll get it.

He went through the burlap flaps. The draft
enveloped the kid in strains of Verdi and the exotic
odors of Ichy's dinner. The candy bar
was in the kid's pocket quicker than Ichy returned.

But Mr. Ichstein, the kid said, I can't make change
for a ten. No worry kid, said Ichy, it's Christmas time.

Carl Wolf

His Crocus Hill custom required more
of Carl Wolf than the mending and hemming of clothes.
Carl was a listener, a safe-keeper of secrets
who dwelt in the confessional darkness of his shop
at Grand and Oxford, across from Vince's Pure Oil.

His eyes, those of a bird wary of predators
from the sky; his head, a tonsured Saxon monk's.
Would he say so little for shame of his immigrant English
or for the threads he'd always be cutting with his teeth?
No one cared, as long as no one but Carl was listening.

Could you fix her high school uniform so she won't show
till June? You'd know best who'd need my Robert's clothes.
But what of Carl, where was he to take
his secrets, his screaming dreams of crematoria?
Not to his wife, not to his daughter or to his son.

They'd stayed behind, in the indistinguishable
ashes of his house in Dresden. So where was Carl
to go, if not to the hard promise of a psalm:
Let my tongue cleave to the roof of my mouth
if ever I should forget you.

The Title Game

Again the seminal season and fungoed moonshots
pause above the gloves tracking them before
the school wall in right. Infield finished
our kids sprint out there for the title game.

Two of our kids are riding the far end
of the bench. They're dreaming of girls and Nook burgers;
they joke about the old guys in worn-out loafers
lined up there behind the wrought-iron fence

on Randolph. The one with his foot on the fence rail nudges
his buddy when our kid lines home a run in the third:
Schmidty's grandson, he says, young Eddie's boy.
Yes, and didn't young Eddie marry a Melady?

The dreaming carries one kid off to the back seat of
his buddy's moon-lit Ford and the sweet wet heat
in the lake night air, the scent of alyssum in her hair.
The dreaming brings the other a walk-off homer.

With our kids down one in the fifth, the old guys seem
to remember this game: You took second on the balk.
Yes, and when their coach came out for a jaw
at the ump, Warner got you up to hit for Monk.

But for all the pensive spitting into the cleat-clawed dirt
we're still down one, two out, and Muff's been sitting
on second for something like sixty years, it seems.
So Jimmy goes to his bench for a kid with a dream in the

bottom of the seventh. Better to hear than to feel
your hit. As their kid tracks it toward the wall in right,
the old guys remember this small May moon in a steel
blue sky, this arc of hope in its seamless flight.

Peto

Saturday afternoon I walked out in my yard.
Kids yelling Not it! and laughing round the tree
Attacked me: Can we help Daddy with the screens?
And they chased one another across the lawn –
Except red-haired Peto – our Collie had him pinned.
How serene Peto was, how like his mother.

Not that our Collie had pinned Peto's mother
Of course; but in springtime, working in the yard
Wearing my letter jacket, her red hair pinned
Up, she'd wash storms I set against the tree.
And today, Peto was a year. By now the lawn
Was strewn with garden tools, kindling wood and screens.

Can I spray, Daddy? Please can I spray the screens?
Patsy sprayed the screens, her friends, her friends' mother
Who was across the hedges raking her lawn.
Now me! And Jeff sprayed Patsy out of the yard.
Look, Daddy, look: there's a bluejay in the tree!
Ha! laughed Hankie, Collie still has Peto pinned.

Not it! Off they raced for a tail to be pinned
On a donkey. A squirrel fled across the screens
The bluejay pillaged a wren's nest in the tree
And little Tom Cobb cried, because his mother
Spanked him for letting down his pants in the yard.
Peto watched me pull our hose across the lawn.

Across the alley, stretched bathing on their lawn
Lay Fred Healey's wife, ivory limbs pinned
By the sun to prickly grass. Quickly the yard
Filled up again with shrieks and shouts for more screens
To spray and Collies' ears to pull. A mother
Called and I was left with only mine. The tree

Was hiding Jeff from Patsy's cry, and the tree
Was propping Peto up upon the lawn
(Its dark oak bark; the red hair of his mother)
One, two, three on Jeffrey! Then they all three pinned
Their Collie in the sun. Unmindful of screens
That hung on hallow walls, I stood in my yard

Near the tree, where, deep in lawn, those other screens
Appeared – dark yards of scrim, a year ago pinned
By nurses round the bed of Peto's mother.

The Tutor

You thought it was only they
who needed the flight
of your canny mouth,
your lighting on the rim of their world
wings spread over them
eclipsing the sun in their needy eyes,
your meeting the thrusts
of their featherless throats
all agape in a chorus of more.

The Wake

He said he'd send for her and their child within
and the wake began – as they always did – with the giddy
gossoons clowning ahead of their elders along
the mud-rutted boreen that wound down from Clashmore
to the River Blackwater. The scent of salmon and seaweed
now on the evening air replaced the smell of dung
and potatoes rotting in the village fields above.

He said he'd send for her and their child within
when his parents, Mike and Meg, his Mary and the others
carried their fare and firewood down to the landing
the women with baskets of bread and turnips, the men
with wheelbarrows of wood and crocks of ale.
Freddy Malins, screwed on his own poitin, was seen
taking Colleen Boyle behind the boathouse.

He said he'd send for her and their child within
when night set in and the villagers raised their jars to him
and sang round the fire those melancholy, coffin-ship
send-for-me songs, and cried from too much grief or drink.
By dawn the villagers had gone. His parents and his Mary
would take him – him with his rucksack and tool belt – over
the river, then down to Cobh to board the ship.

Other Poems

"On a Rooftop in Fallujah" and "Bletchley Park" were written after Jane and I saw the Oscar-nominated movies *American Sniper* and *The Imitation Game* in California in the winter of 2015.

"Helen of Tuscumbia" is a "found poem." A found poem is one in which the author imports into the poem passages from the writings of one or more other authors. The borrowed text may be incorporated wholesale, or it may be edited. Authors of found poems of course credit their original sources. In this poem, I have borrowed significant parts of a letter written by Helen Keller from her home in Tuscumbia, Alabama to her host at the Chicago World's Fair in 1893. I have also imported lines from T.S. Eliot's "The Waste Land" (lines 3-5 in the third stanza). The personification of April in "Eveline" (page 8) is also borrowed from Eliot.

The haiku about flowers and forgetfulness was a winner of Public Art St. Paul's 2011 Sidewalk Poetry contest. It is imprinted in sidewalk panels in several parts of the city, including in front of our house at 468 Holly Ave.

The "Thanksgiving 2008" sonnet was inspired by my admiration of granddaughters Caroline and Mary Murphy. I wrote the villanelle "The Belles of St. Bart's" to honor my granddaughters Molly and Norah Murphy.

"Duvida" was written in 2014, the centennial of Teddy Roosevelt's bold but recklessly dangerous voyage down a tributary of the Amazon River in Brazil. Material in the poem was taken from Candice Millard's great book on the subject, *The River of Doubt*. *Duvida* is the Portuguese word for doubt.

Buddy

Buddy imagines himself a whiskered
Edwardian, always dressed for his meals
in black coat and tail, carrying himself
from room to room as fortune's heir: brow high
back straight, a purpose to his club man's gait.

His is a scientist's soul, or a poet's,
drawn – as his kind will be – to the hard work
of scratching for the truth behind closed doors,
sometimes succeeding (as when he wakes me
from my nap) sometimes not (the pantry door).

Like most well-bred, highbrow Edwardians
Buddy appears to have read his Kipling;
he seems to know that success and failure
are both impostors, that truth never lies
behind closed doors but in his trying them.

Polonius Takes the Putt

Imagine his astonishment, Laertes'
standing off the ninth green with his old man
Polonius, and the other two gentlemen
who fill the Saturday foursome, all sweating
like cantered horses beneath the heat-indexed
sun of July. They take water. Report scores.

Polonius, an officer of the court, sworn
to uphold its principles of justice and truth,
has done all that and more: He's made a mole
of his daughter, Ophelia, and spied on Prince
Hamlet, all for the good of the state.
So, for the likes of Polonius, nearing retirement

that putt had seemed a harmless preemption.
In his flaccid flesh all speckled brown with age
years of riding at arms and the politics of court
he hides now from the sun beneath his great Tam.
His needs are simple, but they are urgent: water,
a son's respect, one measly par for the nine.

He'd taught his son to ride, to fence, to follow
the rules of chivalry and golf, sent him off to college
with that last precept: *To thine own self be true,*
for thou canst not then be false to any man.
Except, perhaps, by pocketing that two-footer
but telling your son you'd sunk the putt for par.

And now imagine his astonishment, Laertes'
just home from college for the funeral, when Hamlet
passes along to him the old man's
dying words, *Give my son this corollary*
to that last precept: When you fall from your horse
don't blame the horse. And do remount.

On a Rooftop in Fallujah

The lens carries his eye to myriad scenes
like the moon at dusk with its little sidekick Venus
looking up to it as if the moon were its mother

or perhaps there in the shadows on the moon
he sees the Madonna gazing down upon the Child
knowing the sweetness of this moment won't last

or does the lens carry him back now
to his own childhood, the piano in the convent parlor
the warmth of Sister Agnes' hands covering his

or is he seeing again from his bedroom window
the young mother in her bathroom across the alley
using her towel first to dry her little boy?

But surely he must see by now that the lens
reveals neither moon, Madonna, nun nor neighbor
and nothing like a vision of his own wife and boy.

Surely he sees by now the peril in his sights:
a burka'd woman and her child sent out to bomb
the convoy he's on a rooftop in Fallujah to protect.

Bletchley Park

For each ecstatic instant
We must an anguish pay
In keen and quivering ratio
To the ecstasy. Emily Dickinson

If we've learned anything at all from the Greeks,
Oedipus to Aeschylus, Aesop to Icarus
it's this: Go ahead, wait till all your chickens
have hatched to get a dependable count;
you'll still end up with egg on your face.

Take Zeno's second paradox, for example:
His theorem proves that the proud, fleet-heeled
Achilles did not, after all, overtake the tortoise.
Or Daedalus, brilliant as his wing design was,
lost his giddy, golden son to pilot error.

And now to Bletchley Park, where cryptologists
mingling the ganglia of their dreaming minds
with the wires, algorithms, levers and cycles
of their Ultra machine, breached the Enigma code.
At last, they'd save the convoys, at glorious last.

At least they'd save some, the lucky ones Ultra's
cycles chose not to sacrifice as bloody bait
to mask the breach. So, how Pyrrhic the glory
for the cryptologist who lost his blue-eyed son,
Isaac, a deck-hand on a ship sacrificed by Ultra.

White Caps

Well, white caps, perhaps
long ago
but now frozen in time
ice-aged
cold with indifference,
not so
they swell up to meet me
moon drawn
raising some pale hope
of rescue;
rather it is I who sails
down to them
to slam and to slam
yet again
upon their dumb shoulders
and wonder
to see in the bluest of skies
a pair of skis
poles too, criss-crossed
thrust upward
as in desperate supplication
to a moon
pale above the white mountain.

Helen of Tuscumbia

Hers was no ordinary thank-you note to a host
at the 1893 World's Fair in Chicago.
You shouldn't be surprised, says Helen, at the beauty
God reveals through the eyes of the mind and soul.
See how sightless Oedipus could lead his daughters
to his final resting place, the grove in Colonus.

I am like one with eyes in her fingers, she says,
who spies beauty, takes it, presses it to her heart.
I am in a beautiful place with the wind rushing
through tall trees; a sound like the sea at high tide.
And so the sea must have sounded to blind Gloucester
rescued by his son on the cliffs above Dover.

As evening falls, she says, the tall trees
send me the murmuring sound of the sea at low tide.
And so Tiresius, blind and throbbing between
two lives, an old man with wrinkled breasts
saw the evening hour that strives toward home
and heaves the sailor home from the sea.

The summer is feeling very rich now, she says
his golden fruits are ripening fast
and the roadsides gleam with goldenrod.
I can see all this here in Tuscumbia just as clearly
as any exhibit at the Fair, for I see the beauty
of God's world in my fingers, mind and soul.

Deconstruction

It's the first one you'll see on the left
just past the hostess in his black
floor-length gown, offering wine.

On an azure canvas, a white sail,
its insignia: a violin, strings to the wind
damaged beyond repair; or perhaps

a raquet smashed on a net post
by a tennis brat or long-haired lovers
with wines scented of oak or arsenic;

two blood-red rivulets, bar sinister
evidence of anger and its spawn
traversed by yellow pencils of sunlight

no doubt to expose the madness of it all.
And beneath it, the title: "Deconstruction"
then Greenberg-Flynn-Phlaum, an artist

suffering a crisis of self-identity
or a post-modern *ménage à trois*.
Then the red dot: either a careless drop

of blood spilled from the red rivulets
or a sign the U.N. diplomat from Mali
has bought this thing for a giddy mil.

Six Seasonal Haiku

I can't remember
all the flowers she taught me
Her pansies worry

Our oak tree's last leaves
will stay till the carolers
come and sing for them.

With her Strauss waltz glide
on the moonlit ice, my love
skates past me to hers.

The proud cardinal
must compete with new colors.
Winter's snow is gone.

To hear a silence
like your yard when the hawk comes,
turn off your TV.

The Little League son
I used to take to Twins games
now buys the tickets.

Thanksgiving 2008

When I bring back Thanksgiving 2008
in the white, hill-high house near the bend in the street,
I see Caroline and Mary follow their Kate
to the kitchen and back with this tray full of treats
she sets before the hearth, where laughter from the flames
lights the eyes of little girls in gowns of deep blue;
yes, little laughing eyes like Pleiades framing
the darkness of that starry night Van Gogh knew.

It's time now time for the girls' story, the one their Tim
asks them to read us – about the naughty parrot
who shapes up quick when carried to the fridge, wherein
the headless turkey waits beside the cooked carrots.

Then, gathered round the table, we ask God to bless
us all and, yes, John Patrick and Tynan Thomas.

The Belles of St. Bart's

As Molly came first with her something to ring,
like the bells in St. Bart's or the news of her sister,
Norah would wait till the gnomes wish to sing.

In the font at St. Bart's, where the Jordan was flowing,
Molly led Norah through their blessings of water,
As Molly came first with her something to ring.

On Grandparents' Day, and the kids all careering,
little Norah would linger with us; it's no bother:
Norah would wait till the gnomes wish to sing.

When the organ was cued and the bells began chiming,
the plaid and candled choir would all enter.
As Molly came first with her something to ring

fay Norah would linger with us, listening
to the hymns, and making us guess whether
Norah would wait till the gnomes wish to sing.

They're the belles of St. Bart's, this blending of being;
allegro and adagio, one listening for the other.
As Molly came first with her something to ring
Norah would wait till the gnomes wish to sing.

Duvida

Duvida, Duvida, you counsel against killing
these rude intruders who hack, crash and curse
their crude portages around all the bouldered falls
along our rain-drowned river that snakes
a thousand miles down to the Amazon.

At night, Duvida, they'd neither see nor hear us coming
in our bare feet on the alluvial floor of the forest
quick and quiet as jaguars to surround their camp;
the last sounds they'd hear: the river, the snoring
of their jowly, mustachioed Colonel with the pince-nez

and, no doubt, the war cry of the Cinta Larga.
Their guns would be useless in close quarters against
our poisoned arrows and rock-honed blades.
If we don't kill them now, Duvida, when they are weak
with the fevers of the forest, scarce food, bad water

boats battered, arguing among themselves;
if we don't kill them now, Duvida, if we let them pass
they'll be back again to take our forest
like the rubber tree men along the Amazon
like the telegraph men across the Mato Grosso.

But you stay our arms, Duvida, our stealth and strength
against these risks. You see the rude intruders
as passersby, not land thieves, not yet;
so you tell us, for all twenty of them dead tonight, you'd
not risk the life of a single Cinta Larga.

But Duvida, Duvida, in the time of our fathers
the Nhambiquara also let those first
intruders pass along the Amazon
across the Mato Grosso, only to see them
return with the takers, the rubber and telegraph men.

The Swan

Though not at all schooled in ballet
I can promise you this

the price of a ticket up close
is worth every cent

to watch the white swan swim across
the stage in her lace dress and slippers
tacking diagonally toward me
the strings of Tchaikovsky surrounding us

her ivory neck and limbs
arc leftward then swoon off to the right
like boughs of birch trees waving
to one another across a lake

or perhaps, as in a silent film
with one wing she may now be feathering
a cocktail table
and then, with the other, perhaps lifting up
or setting down a crystal glass

before she arrives at the edge of the stage
bends deeply before me
as a courtesan might, inviting me
to gaze upon her where I will

inviting this exchange of whispered secrets
between us, perhaps a kiss, her face now
so close I breathe the very scent of her
and see in her inviting eyes

the promise she has surely made to me
before she turns her smile away
and exits, stage right, leaving me there
to long for her return

and when she does, to keep her promise
she wakes me to the denouement of her dance
by placing my check next to my glass
a reminder that my white swan

is a cocktail waitress
at the Slavyanskaya Hotel in Moscow

presenting her name to me once more
to gaze upon, to wonder at: Odette

Silver Lake

Was that our Charlie who was just here
My love
With his little girls
Their thumbs pistoning away in their laps
Heads bent over their whole worlds
Until it was time for their dad to take them home?

And wasn't it our Charlie who at their age
My love
Would sit with us of a summer evening
The scent of alyssum in the still air
Watching the daylight fade behind the hills
Across Silver Lake?

And the neighbor's chocolate Lab
My love
Wouldn't she come down to the lake at sundown
To send her baleful calls across to the hills
And take the echoes as an answer
from her missing mate?

Surely you can hear now how I depend on you
My love
To sort these things out for me
As daylight fades outside our bay window
Where I watch Charlie and the girls drive away
Where I listen again now for you.

The Little Sisters of the Poor

will demur and tell you that anyone
could change out the old men's
linens, wash, towel and salve their
bed-sore limbs all in a wordless
motion; that anyone with a sturdy
pair of oxfords and a wool shawl
to shoulder through December's snow
could take the Sisters' beggar steps
to the shops along West Seventh.

and Songs

I composed "Acacia Memory" for Jane on our 35th wedding anniversary and sang it to her in the dining room at Stout's Island Lodge in Mikana, Wisconsin. The melody is from "When You and I Were Young, Maggie;" and the lyrics are a blend of my own verses with refrains from "Maggie" and from Sean O'Casey's adaptation of that song for his play "The Plow and the Stars." I changed the title to this familiar tune to "Acacia Memory," after the name of a park on a hill overlooking the Minnesota River south of downtown St. Paul, near where the Minnesota and Mississippi rivers merge.

My brother Bill died in 2009. I gave the eulogy at his memorial Mass. One of the themes I developed in the eulogy drew from the folk ballad, Billy Boy," about the charming young bachelor who courts a lass who can bake a cherry pie, but who may be too young to marry just yet. After the funeral, I composed these lyrics to go with the melody of "Billy Boy." Bill's children and I sing this song together at our annual luncheon to remember their father, charming Billy.

I composed "Catherine's Song" for my daughter's wedding in 2001 and sang it to her at the reception. The melody is borrowed from the famous Irish ballad "Grace."

Most colleges and many high schools will have two school songs: a pep song for sports events or rallies and an anthem for more formal occasions, like graduations or alumni gatherings. Cretin-Derham Hall inherited Cretin's peppy "Rouser" when Cretin and Derham Hall merged in 1987. But the schools have never had an anthem. So in the run-up to the 50th reunion of my Cretin class of 1957, I composed the lyrics and melody for "The Occasional." The music was "arranged" by Axel Theimer and Brian Campbell, music professors at St. John's University in Collegeville, Minnesota. It was presented to the school as a gift from our class at our reunion in 2007. The version of "The Occasional" that you will hear on the CD accompanying this book was recorded in Collegeville by the St. John's Men's Chorus.

Acacia Memory

Remember the hill o'er the river, Janie,
The place years ago we lingered long.
You brought the bread and your smile, Janie,
and I brought the wine and a song.

They say now we're aging and gray, Janie,
The raising of children proudly done;
So let's sing to the days that are gone, Janie,
When you and I were young.

The lilacs perfumed all the hill, Janie,
And the shade of the green linden tree,
Where I first said I'd love only you, Janie.
And you said you'd love only me.

And now we are aging and gray, Janie.
The trials of troth are all but done;
So let's sing to the days that are gone, Janie,
When you and I were young.

The breeze through the trees sang us a song, Janie,
Of times you and I were yet to see,
When I first said I'd love only you, Janie,
And you said you'd love only me.

They say we are aging and gray, Janie.
As spray from a great lake's waves are flung;
But to me you're as fair as you were, Janie,
When you and I were young.

Yes, to me you're as fair as you were, Janie,
Years ago when our song had just begun.

Billy's Song

Oh where have you gone
Billy Boy, Billy Boy?
Oh where have you gone
Charming Billy?
He had gone to seek a wife
And the joy of his life.
She was a young thing
And could not leave her mother.

Could she bake a cherry pie
Billy Boy, Billy Boy?
Could she bake a cherry pie
Charming Billy?
She could bake a cherry pie
In the twinkling of an eye.
She was a young thing
And could not leave her mother.

So the rhythm went around
As it will, Billy Boy;
So the rhythm went around
Charming Billy.
You sang us songs and took a chance
You were there to lead our dance.
Now you've gone Bill,
There'll never be another.

Will we miss your laugh and smile
Billy Boy, Billy Boy?
Will we miss your laugh and smile
Charming Billy?
Yes we'll miss your laugh and smile
And yarns you spun us by the mile.
You may be gone Bill,
But you, we will, remember.

You may be gone now Bill,
But you, we will, remember.

Catherine's Song

First Verse:
As we gather on your wedding day
Dear Catherine tears do flow;
If more for joy than sadness though
I simply cannot say.
You had been my Little Strawberry;
I'd taught you how to ride.
Now here you are this fine man's bride,
Your youth, my reverie.

Refrain:
Oh Catherine how the seasons turn.
Where is my baby daughter –
The girl who climbed into my arms to cry?
A woman now, with your own home
And the wish for children's laughter;
A kiss of joy is shared tonight with tears of sweet goodbye.

Second Verse:
I had sent you wobbling on your bike
Down Linden Hills one morn,
And you returned with pigtails shorn
All dressed for prom that night.
But you gave me time to ride with you
Through Shorewood's meadowed hills;
We cantered past the old windmill
Toward futures neither knew.

Refrain:
Oh Catherine how the seasons turn, etc.

Third Verse:
When you left your Northfield college green
We met in Dublin town.
With Titian hair and long green gown
Sure you looked the Irish queen;
As you did again today when we
Walked down that sacred aisle.
'Twas like a Gandolf trip for me
To watch your radiant smile.

Refrain:
Oh Catherine how the seasons turn, etc.

A kiss of joy is shared tonight with tears of sweet goodbye.

The Occasional

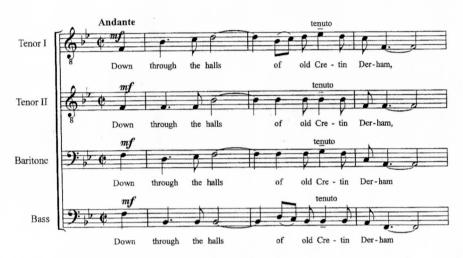

The Occasional

(an anthem for Cretin-Derham Hall)

First Verse:
Down through the halls of Cretin-Derham
flow memories of our school days gone.
Echoes of laughter heard from classrooms filled with sun;
warmed were the friendships that lasted so long.

When we marched down the field
we held cross and colors high.
We learned to be loyal,
to fear never yield.

Second Verse:
Down from the walls of old Cretin-Derham
gaze classes proud of honors they passed along.
Their joys and sorrows, all the heartaches overcome,
parade there before us, remembered in song.

From the purple hue of dawn
till the fall of golden days,
from the proudest halls and fields
we Raiders shall march on!

Before he became a lawyer, Michael E. Murphy taught English at St. Olaf College and Macalester College. He began his thirty-year career as an international business lawyer with Medtronic in 1975 and, in 1980, joined the Minneapolis law firm of Faegre & Benson (now Faegre Baker Daniels) to start the firm's international practice. He retired from Faegre at the end of 2004 and, since then, has been teaching a class on The Law in Literature at the University of St. Thomas School of Law. He lives in St. Paul with his wife, Jane Randolph Murphy, a loyal alum of The Academy of Holy Angels and St. Catherine University. Mike and Jane have four children and six grandchildren, all living in the Twin Cities area.

Michael Murphy's Songs of Crocus Hill *provides just what its title suggests it will: a music that arises from a particular place. Many, most, of these are "memory poems," but by no means sentimental: in his care for language and form, Murphy's* Crocus Hill *pulls off the magic of the best autobiographical writing, somehow enlarging us by narrowing our focus. He has taken to heart Yeats's dictum that the merely personal "soon rots; it must be packed in ice or salt." These tightly packed poems will travel well.*

– James Silas Rogers, editor of *New Hibernia Review*

Crocus Hill comes lyrically into our perception through the Irish, Catholic, Classical undertones of Michael Murphy, scholar and poet. He breathes the essence of his life's stories into a legacy for family and friends, as well as the general readership. He charms us with classical references and disarms us with memories, deliciously served as slices of life. We applaud Michael's talent for the particular – observations most of us might fail to see – and for his poetic prowess, mixing traditional verse forms with the new, freer styles. This is a fine legacy for us all, summoning our own love of the quotidian alongside the extraordinary days of our being. Thank you, Michael, for sharing this creative and poignant endeavor.

– Dorothea Bisbas, Poet Laureate, Rancho Mirage, California

Michael – Today being John's birthday I am reflecting lots and that brings me to say to you that Cate has shared with me a packet of your poetry. I want you to know that if J could have read them I know, full well, that he would find them so very fine and be so proud that you are using your exceptional gift for making poems of beauty and grace...and love. I think the same...some take my breath away. Love, S.

– Sandra Murphy, wife of John Murphy

Published 2015, Saint Paul, Minnesota.

Special thanks to my wife, Jane, for her patient and perceptive editing eye.
She has listened to and read and re-read these poems with me over the years,
always giving me honest and useful critiques.

Typeset by Cate Murphy.